Pamela Goodall has had many psychic and spiritual experiences happened to her throughout her life. She has owned a spiritual shop in the past, has a meditation group, gives card readings, provides workshops, gives talks on spirituality and channels messages from higher beings. She has self-published three books containing many channellings. She has channelled many paintings, which may become an oracle card set. She is a caring person who lives in the beautiful South West of England. Pamela works for love, light and peace and channels universal love that we may interact peacefully with each other.

I dedicate this book to my loving family, friends and all who work in the Light of Source.

Pamela Jean Goodall

DRAWN TO THE LIGHT

AUSTIN MACAULEY PUBLISHERS™
LONDON • CAMBRIDGE • NEW YORK • SHARJAH

All of the events in this memoir are true to the best of author's memory. The views expressed in this memoir are solely those of the author.

A CIP catalogue record for this title is available from the British Library.

ISBN 9781398472020 (Paperback)
ISBN 9781398472037 (ePub e-book)

www.austinmacauley.com

First Published 2023
Austin Macauley Publishers Ltd®
1 Canada Square
Canary Wharf
London
E14 5AA

I acknowledge and thank all those who have allowed me to share their stories and also those who took their time to read this book and make helpful comments.

Table of Contents

Chapter 1: The Early Years 11

Chapter 2: Infants and Juniors 17

Chapter 3: High School 24

Chapter 4: Good Times 31

Chapter 5: Spiritual Family 38

Chapter 6: Starting Work 43

Chapter 7: A Hard Time 46

Chapter 8: A Full-Time Mum 51

Chapter 9: Dark Times 54

Chapter 10: Ordinary and Extraordinary Times 57

Chapter 11: Annis Horriblis 61

Chapter 12: Single but Happy 67

Chapter 13: Getting Connected 72

Chapter 14: My Path at Last 79

Chapter 1
The Early Years

So let me start at the beginning. I was born in 1946, the year of the bulge. Why the bulge? It was because World War II had just ended and the men had come home, so the ladies' stomachs were bulging and there was a large bulge in the birth rate. According to my baby book I was born at 2:45 in the morning on December 6 and I was a big baby, 9 lbs 5 oz – a veritable monster.

I was a lucky child, having loving parents and an older sister, Evelyn. She was four years older than me and had been born during the Second World War in 1942.

Me, Mum, Eve, Dad and Goldie, our dog, in front of the air raid shelter in the back garden.

From my baby book it says that I crawled at nine months, took my first step at 11 months, walked at 12 months and climbed at 16 months. My mother's comment was: "Later than Evelyn at walking, but very forward with talking."

Evidently, my first holiday was when I was eight months old and we all went on the train to Leigh-on-Sea in Essex to visit my Nanny and Grampa. I went again to Leigh-on-Sea when I was two, because my sister and I were bridesmaids at my Uncle Ernie's wedding to Aunt Hilda. Evidently during the ceremony, I wandered down the aisle singing *Away in a Manger* and then *Tinker Tailor.* I do not remember this, but I know our dresses were made of light blue satin with frills around, as I can remember dressing up in them when I was older.

With my teddy in the back garden behind the garage.

At two years of age, I repeated prayers and loved to say Amen. Evidently, in the middle of my prayer, I would look up and say 'Jesus loves me'. I started Sunday School by three years of age and by the time I was $3^1/_2$ I knew The Lord's Prayer almost perfectly.

Evidently, I was a very contented child and could amuse myself for long periods. Our family had a dog Goldie and cat Tiddles and when I was 18 months my parents started keeping chickens. I loved all animals and when I was $3^1/_2$ I was delighted when a litter of baby pigs came into our garden.

We had the ground floor flat in a semi-detached house. In the dining room, there were two built-in cupboards. The one on the right was for my sister Eve's toys and the one on the left was my toy cupboard. The table and chairs were in the middle of the room and I think there were two easy chairs.

The other big room was the bedroom. My mum and dad's bed was in the middle on one wall and Eve's bed and my bed on the opposite wall in the two alcoves on either side of the fireplace. What a squash. Of course, we had the kitchen and an outside toilet. We shared a bathroom with the lady in the upstairs flat.

Some people remember being in their cot or pram as a baby. Not me, for my earliest detailed memory was when I was about three years of age. I loved to sit by my toy cupboard and dress my dolls and especially remember getting my dolly dressed and putting her into my pram and pretending we were going to visit her granny. I would push the pram around the table several times and then went up the hallway. We had to go by bus to Granny's, so I sat with my doll on the stairs pretending that we were on the bus. When I felt we had arrived at my bus stop, I would get off and push my pram down the hallway to the kitchen door. I would knock on the door and my mum would ask who was there. I would say, "It's me and we have come to visit you."

My mum would open the door and welcome us in. I would stay a while asking how she was and what had been happening. Sometimes I helped with baking or washing the dishes. After a short while I would decide it was time to leave and catch the 'bus' back and so would start my journey out of the kitchen, up the hall, onto the stairs and back around the dining room table to home by my toy cupboard.

Sometimes after Eve and I woke, probably Sundays, we would climb into my mum and dad's bed. Often a tickling session would ensue. I don't think I was a vicious child, but I do remember sitting across my dad's stomach and trying to pull a hair out of his hairy chest. I have also been told that as a young child I loved to play with my Great Aunt Jessie's red handbag.

Eve, my sister and I went to Sunday School each Sunday and would walk through Linketty Lane on the way to the Church and back. Often we would pass Basil the tramp, carrying his sack. He was very smelly, but a gentle soul. We would turn into Church Hill and often would meet the cows going back to the local farm. Eve and I would be scared and squash ourselves against the wall to let them pass.

My mum and dad were given the opportunity to buy the house we were living in and did take this opportunity. Mum lived in our family home for over 70 years.

Coming back through the lane I often picked the wild flowers for my mum. Ragged Robin, Milkmaids, Red Campian, Daisies, Primroses, Violets, Bluebells and others, whatever flowers were in season. No one thought at that time that we shouldn't pick wild flowers as they might become rare. My mum would put the flowers in a vase or jam jar on the kitchen windowsill.

Mostly Eve and I got on well, but my mum said that we grew in spasms, because Eve was four years older than me and sometimes grew away from me and then I would catch up with her. So sometimes we played well and sometimes we fought. I can remember having a real punch up with her on the settee, but now I have no idea what it was about.

Chapter 2
Infants and Juniors

I started Infants School when I was four. It was a long way and Mum could only take me and Eve, who was in the Juniors, to the bus stop to catch the school bus. She was not allowed to accompany us and I can remember crying when she left. I had to stay in school for dinner and then we went into the playground for the rest of the dinner hour. Eve was given special permission to come up to the dividing fence between the Infants and Juniors to be with me because I couldn't stop crying. I feel sure that Eve would not be too happy with this arrangement, probably wanting to play with her friends.

One day in my first year at school we were learning to count with a big abacus at the front of the classroom. I knew my numbers, so got bored and started daydreaming out of the class window. Mrs Webber, the teacher came up to scold me and hit me with the ruler across the knuckles, so that I would concentrate. Ouch, it was very painful.

I also remember the class sitting on forms in the school hall. We were singing a song, which I still love to this day.

Daises are our silver,
Buttercups our gold,
This is all the treasure,

We can have or hold.

When I went to Junior School I made a best friend, who lived quite near me. When I walked to her house, it was imperative that I climbed to the top of the hedge in the lane, where children had made a 'secret path' all along the top, even stepping over large roots from the trees.

Me as untidy schoolgirl.

We often walked to school together. We had to pass near to a stream, which was a big attraction to us and we were often late arriving at school or going home and often quite wet. When we learned to ride our bikes, we rode to school, but going home we had to push the bikes up the hills because in those days bikes had no gears.

We loved playing a game we had at school, but I can't remember if there was a name for it. The school was built like the letter E and between the prongs of the building, there was grass. Around the grass on one side was a pathway, which was lower than the grass. It got deeper as it went around and at one place was about six feet deep. Here we dared each other to put our hands across to the other wall, about 2–3 feet. The bigger dare was to put one leg across and no hands holding the far wall.

We also played on the playground railings doing rollovers and hanging by our knees. We also enjoyed playing two ball. In most games, we threw the balls against the wall. I remember playing this game against the wall while chanting to the tune of

"One, two, three, O'Leary".
One two three and PLAINSY
Four five six and PLAINSY
Seven eight nine and PLAINSY
Ten and PLAINSY, catch the ball.
(Followed by the same, substituting
OVER, UPSY and DROPSY)

Often we played skipping, either separately or in a large group with the game 'keep the kettle boiling, never let it stop'. A large rope was turned by two girls and a long line of girls had to run through the rope or jump over it and not get caught in the rope. Another joint skipping game was 'there's somebody under the bed'. When you called the name of another girl to come in with you, you both had to skip the rope. Then when it came to 'get out you fool', the first person had to jump out of the rope.

"There's somebody under the bed
Whoever can it be
It makes me feel so frightened
So xxxx come in with me.
Xxx light the candle
Xxx look under the bed,
Get out you fool, get out you fool,
There's nobody under the bed."

and this one where you had to do what it says.

"Teddy Bear, Teddy Bear, turn around,
Teddy Bear, Teddy Bear, touch the ground
Teddy Bear, Teddy Bear, turn out the light
Teddy Bear, Teddy Bear, say good-night!"
There were lots of single skipping games too.

'Jam tart, strawberry tart, tell me the name of your sweetheart' and then the rope had to be turned faster as you called out 'A B C D' etc until you tripped the rope.

I remember the last line of another game where you shouted, "Salt, Pepper, Mustard Vinegar" and while doing this you had to skip as fast as you could.

I also remember a craze for hula hooping and another where every girl had a tin of beads for swopping, which we called swoppsees. Most precious were the sparkling diamonds in different colours. Sadly, these were not real diamonds as they were made out of glass.

Around our girls' playground was a slope which was grass and when this was cut, we played grass fights and also did roly-polys down the slope. We ended up covered in grass bits but smelling lovely. I still love the smell of freshly cut grass.

One day I was sick and put to bed. In my bedroom was a photo of my nanny and her sister when they were young girls. I called my mum as I was very frightened because I could see that my nanny's sister was talking to me with her mouth moving. I didn't understand this and so my mum removed the photo from the bedroom.

I didn't think I was such a chatterbox, but twice I got hit at school for talking. Once when in the needlework class, I got smacked on the back of the leg at the knee and I also had the cane on my hand in the top class, very painful.

Mr Young was the teacher in the top class and he was very strict, but I remember him with affection. Every week we would have tests such as mental arithmetic, arithmetic, writing and spelling. Where we sat in the class for the next week was dependent on how well we did in these tests.

The top girls sat in the first line of desks, cleverest at the back, not so clever at the front. Second best girls and top boys sat in the next line of desks and so on. I was a second-best girl. The two top boys were both good looking and I was smitten. So I would work really hard so that I got to sit at the back with one of them. The week I was sitting next to one of them, I didn't work too hard and would end up down at the front the following week. But then I would work hard so that the following week I ended up once again at the back. But it seems that working every other week paid off.

At this time my friend and I went to Brownies. I ended up as a Sixer of the Pixies, my friend was in the Elfs. At Brownies, we used to sing

"We're the Brownies
Here's our aim
Lend a hand and
Play the game."

We also learnt new skills and attained badges to sew on our uniforms.

Here I am in the Brownies, I am wearing my beret and peeping through from the second row.

One day while waiting at the bus stop to go home from Brownies with my friend and my mum I remember seeing a ball of fire flying across the sky from west to east. I expect this was a meteorite, but it must have been quite large as to my young eyes it appeared to be bigger than the moon and quite low as it travelled across the sky. My mum thought it probably landed on Dartmoor.

At home Eve and I often played in the garden. Dad was a plasterer and did odd jobs for people, so there were always planks and blocks for building in the garden. We used to make obstacle courses with these, up onto the air raid shelter and down again and balancing along planks. We also used a plank to make a seesaw on the railings beside the garage. Next to our garden was a big bramble patch and we made dens inside the brambles.

I often sat on the air raid shelter using my finger to squash little red spiders that were there and getting red dots on my finger. (Nowadays I don't like to kill anything.)

There were a group of children in the street, mostly around Eve's age. I was allowed grudgingly to tag along with them. One day on November 5 (bonfire night), we went to a friend's house across the road for fireworks. One of the boys sent a wriggly firecracker along the path towards me and it chased me a long way. I was very scared. I think these wriggly fireworks are banned now.

I loved to play two ball against the wall of our house. This must have driven my mum crazy to hear thump thump thump against the wall for hours on end.

Chapter 3
High School

Instead of the 11+ there used to be the Scholarship, which you could pass A or B. If you passed A, then you had a choice to one of the top Grammar Schools. If you passed B then you went to a Grammar School, but which was not quite so good.

When my sister Eve passed the scholarship with an A pass, she was allowed to come home to tell Mum and the story was told of how they danced around the room in delight. I took the scholarship and I was sitting next to one of the best boys when the results were read out. If you had passed you had to stand up. Both my boy heroes were standing having passed A. All the passes for the boys and girls who had passed A had been read out and all the passes for the boys who had passed B. Then the turn came for the girls, who had passed B to be read out.

I thought I hadn't passed so didn't hear my name and the boy next to me had to poke me to tell me to stand. We were allowed to go home and tell our mothers. I rushed home, expecting to dance around the room. Mum was not in. She was next door having a cup of tea with our neighbour, Aunt Helen. I told her my news and she was pleased, but the conditions were not right and we did not dance around the room. I was deeply disappointed.

In September 1956, when I was nine years old I started in the seniors at Public Secondary School for Girls. On the first day I remember being in the classroom of Form 1H and standing at the back on my own, as I was very shy. I looked to the front of the classroom and saw a girl with dark brown plaits standing by the blackboard and talking with several others. I immediately felt as though I already knew her and recognised her and I wanted to be her friend. I was very shy at that time and could not go over and speak. However, she did not want to be my friend until the third year when she, Carol and I became best friends. She is a soul mate and we are still great friends after over 50 years. I know now that you can have many soul mates, male and female.

My mum had permed my hair so that I would feel good when I started school. Unfortunately, it was a disaster and very very curly. With my beret on top, I looked awful as you can see and I was extremely embarrassed.

In my school uniform for 1st year of high school.

Whilst at High School I often went across the road into the Museum either during my dinner hour or after school. I was fascinated and drawn to the case of Egyptian items which was on a landing on the stairs, but first I always had to run past the two mummy cases in the foyer, I always felt scared of them.

At school we did all the usual subjects. I hated sports as we would have to travel in a bus to somewhere else in the city. We went to Central Park for hockey in the winter, playing in our shorts and the weather was really cold. In summer we went to Collins Park for tennis, which I did enjoy and to a park in Efford for athletics. Our sports teacher asked which athletics we would like to practice. I along with other sport haters chose the long jump. This was because the long jump was behind the changing rooms and we could sunbathe and chat, until someone on watch shouted out that our teacher was approaching and then of course we would be practicing long jump.

At our Maths lesson, two girls who were both very clever were excellent at getting our teacher to chat about her previous life as a teacher in a boys boarding school. She told us about one teacher at this school who was quite old and doddery and the boys drilled through a piece of chalk and inserted a red matchstick. When the teacher wrote on the blackboard the match ignited and he was so shocked he threw the chalk with matchstick out of the window, much to the boy's delight. Of course, all this talking may be the reason that Maths is not my best subject.

Our French teacher always had geraniums on the windowsill in her classroom. They had a really strong smell and although I love the look of geraniums I could never have them in a room. She would also make us wash the blackboard at the end of each lesson. I actually liked French and even enjoyed my homework. When it came to GCE time, we first had to pass a mock exam. I along with most of the class passed written French, however for the oral test a French Mademoiselle was brought in. Our teacher spoke Parisian French, this person was from the south of France. She asked us to give directions to different parts of the city, something we had never done in class. Most of us, including me, failed this test as we could not understand her accent nor give brilliant directions. I don't know about the rest of the girls, but I know that Carol and I were both disappointed about not passing and not be able to take the French GCE.

One day the Religious Knowledge teacher (female, single and prissy) and the Science teacher (male and not bad looking) both went into the store cupboard. One of the naughtier girls locked the door on them and we thought this was really funny. They were there for some time until someone heard them shouting. What a laugh.

In Religious Knowledge all we did was read through the bible. The teacher decided on a chapter and we each read one verse out of the Bible when it was our turn. When it wasn't out turn, it is surprising what girls can get up to. In our desks were marbles, food, pinups of pop stars, drawings and many other things. I remember that one girl had a tin of peaches that she was eating.

Our English teacher was known for her temper. One day a girl at the back of the class dropped her sweets, mint imperials and they rolled all over the floor. The teacher threw the blackboard rubber (wood with felt on one side) at the girl. Thankfully she missed.

Our girls school was housed in the same building as the boys school. We had half the bottom floor and the whole of the middle floor and the boys had half the bottom floor and the whole of the top floor. We could look out the middle floor at the boys' playground. Often Carol and I would sneak into the school hall at dinnertime and we would flash a mirror at a boy we fancied, then we would duck down and giggle. As we got older we girls used to lean out of the toilet windows to talk to the boy prefects at the gate below or just to peer at the ones we fancied.

Fashion at school was always changing and we girls tried to keep up. In the winter-time Carol was in fashion with a pleated skirt and poodle socks. Whereas I won the fashion contest in summer as my mum had made my school dresses as shirt waisters and each week she would wash and starch them. Wow, did I feel good?

In winter there always seemed to be snow and every year the sledge came out of the garage. I remember happy times sledging with my dad, Eve and my Uncle Len (who lived with us) down steep Linketty Lane.

When Carol and I were 15 it really snowed hard in the night, so no buses were running to take us to school. I wrapped up warm and set off walking to Carol's across the valley. She joined me and we enjoyed walking to school in the snow. When we finally got there, we found that they had closed the school as the water pipes had burst. We were very happy to turn around and walk back again.

While we were walking back to Carol's house at Higher Compton and we met her mother, who explained that Carol had been accepted as an apprentice hairdresser and was to start on Monday. Carol never came back to school.

I did one more year at school doing a secretarial course. Our short male form teacher wore a gabardine raincoat and a beret to school. One day some of the girls sewed up the arms of the gabardine and put it with his beret on top of the window pole (used to open and close the top windows and about seven or eight feet long). When he came to get his gabardine and beret instead of just letting the pole go sideways to get them, he started jumping up and down trying to reach. We thought this was extremely funny. Then, when he had worked out how to get his clothes down, he tried to put on his gabardine and couldn't work out why his arms wouldn't go through the sleeves. Hilarious.

During this year the school uniform changed, instead of berets to wear, there were boaters. In our class there was a blackboard on an A frame, this became the wigwam for the Indians and the girls who had boaters were the cowboys. We were having a wonderfully noisy game when the headmistress opened the door. "What are you doing?" she asked. "Playing cowboys and Indians miss," said one of the girls. "Oh," she said and went back to her gin and playing cards in her office.

Chapter 4
Good Times

I was confirmed into the Church of England when I was 13. As the Bishop put his hands on my head, I felt very strong energy going into my head. This was a very spiritual experience for me, something I have never forgotten.

Me dressed for my confirmation into the Church of England.

When I was a child, I saw as a child – innocently. As a young teenager I loved going to our local church, St Edward's in Eggbuckland, Plymouth. While at Communion one Sunday I was singing away with everyone else in praise of the Lord, when I saw movement in the rafters. I knew that this was an angel singing along with us.

We enjoyed family picnics with grandparents, aunts, uncles and cousins, especially on Easter Monday when everyone would gather at our house. When everyone had arrived we would set off walking to Plymbridge for our picnic. Surrounded by trees and splashing in the water by the weir we had great fun. There was also the slate slide, made of natural pieces of slate, just slipping down the hillside. This seemed enormously long to me when young, but perhaps it wasn't so far. However it was a short cut to our picnic spot and all the family would slide down. Wheeee! I also have fond memories of one tree on the riverbank which had wonderful roots and I knew that it was a fairy castle and fairies lived there.

Dad had a motorbike and sidecar and most years we would set off on our annual holidays, all the way to Southend where my Nanny and Grampa lived.

Eve, me and my doll posing for photo on Dad's motorbike

As soon as we could, after arriving in Southend, my sister Evelyn and I would run down to stand on the bridge over the railway, especially when a steam train went through. I loved the Guinness clock, the fair called the Kersaal and walking the mile long pier. What I didn't like was the smell when we went to cockle sheds at Leigh-on-Sea where they sold shellfish. To this day I don't like the smell of shellfish and can't eat it.

I am in the foreground in socks and school blazer, the only jacket I had. My sister, Grampa and Dad behind me. We are standing on the bridge waiting for a steam train to go underneath.

On one journey it was raining hard and we all got extremely cold, as Mum was on the back of the motorbike and there was no heating in the sidecar for me and Eve. Dad stopped by the side of the road and got us to do the Fairy Elephant Dance, stamping around as fast as we could to get warm.

When the raspberries in the garden were ripe I remember coming home from school and picking enough to fill my bowl for tea. My mum used to boil the milk (no refrigerator – how old I feel saying that) and skim the cream from the top. So I was lucky to have raspberries, sugar and cream for my tea. Yummy! When I told a friend in later life, she thought we must have been really posh to have raspberries and cream for tea in the summer.

My mum was a Girl Guide Captain and Eve had become a Tawny Owl for Brownies, I became a Girl Guide after leaving the Brownies. I had to go camping every year with my mum. I did not like camping. We had no integral groundsheet fixed to the tent, just the groundsheet on the ground. We had to make our beds using three blankets and blanket pins for there were no sleeping bags. One night I woke up, switched on my torch and found the groundsheet had moved under my sleeping space. I found I was sleeping on worms and screamed, waking the whole camp.

Eve Tawny Owl, Mum Girl Guide Captain and me Girl Guide.

At camp.
I am on the right in the white blouse and dark hair.

I tried to be one of the naughtiest guides so that the other girls would not think I was a favourite due to my mum being the Captain. I can remember my friend and I going to the shop on the corner and buying 10 cigarettes and matches. Then we would go to the park and smoke the lot before we went to Guides. I know that I felt pretty sick after smoking all those cigarettes.

When I was older and had left guiding behind, I visited my mum's Guide Camp with my dad. We had to cross a field to get to the field they were camped in. It had been raining and suddenly I looked down and the field was covered in slugs. Not liking slimy creatures I jumped onto a small rock and wouldn't move. My dad very kindly gave me a piggyback ride to the camp, where I don't think I moved off the groundsheet.

At my cousin Les's 21st birthday party (I would have been about 17) there was a game where if you lost you had a forfeit and had to wear a piece of clothing. Other people got hats, scarves, skirts, shirts, etc. What did I get – long johns. Everyone thought it hilarious, including me.

The following photo was put up on the notice board by my uncle in my office with the caption 'Winter draws (drawers) on'. It was a good thing I could laugh at myself.

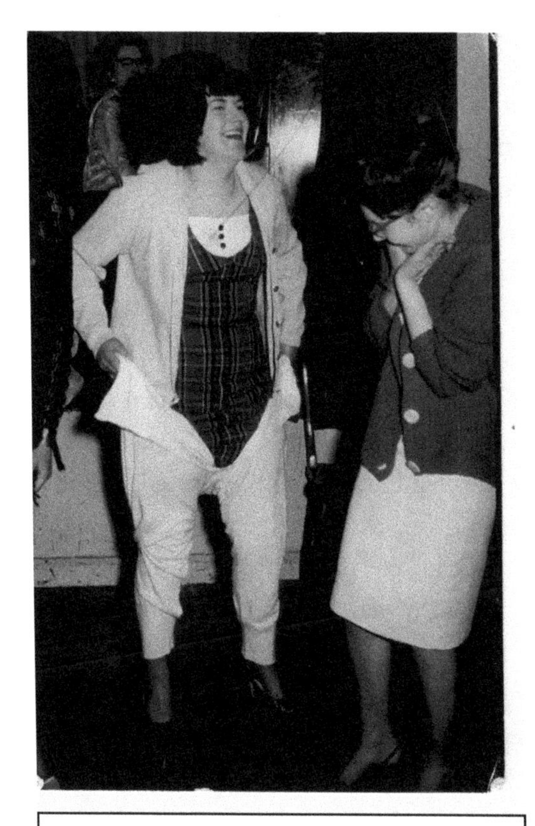

My sister Eve is looking on.

Chapter 5
Spiritual Family

Our house was full of love and both my parents were spiritual (although they probably would not have called themselves that). I know there were many loving spirits within the house and visiting it. Although as a child I didn't see anything, I used to get scared because I felt spirit but didn't understand. I always thought there was someone in my bedroom, especially at the end of my bed and wanted to have a nightlight. I frequently had feelings of not being alone – sometimes being afraid and sometimes not.

My mum sensed spirits and knew when an old lady, who had died, visited our house. She knew it was this lady, because she always visited in the same way, by coming in and out of the back door.

Goldie our dog had died. After this Mum said she saw him running in front of her like a young puppy when she was returning from Crownhill village shops.

When Dad was a young lad, he and his best mate Harry decided to go to a Spiritual Church and poke fun. They stood at the back and at the end of the session the medium spoke to Harry saying that she saw a lady standing behind him. She described this lady and it was Harry's mother. (His mother had been ill and had just died while they were there).

This turned them from sceptics to believers and my dad and Harry decided to practice ESP (thought transference) and they became extremely good. So much so that if they had decided to meet somewhere and one couldn't make it to that destination, he would send a message by ESP to meet elsewhere and maybe change the time of meeting and then they would both arrive at the new destination and at the correct time.

They made a pact that the first to die would come and speak with the other. Harry died in the 1950s in Australia and he and Dad often contacted each other. So much so, that my mum told me that she asked Dad to stop talking to Harry as it kept her awake at night.

I remember one dinnertime we were all sitting around the table and Dad had a photo of a group of people. He said he could see a spirit dog in the photo. I remember looking and looking but still could not see the dog. I would love to find that photo now and look in a different way.

My mum became pregnant when I was 14. As Mum was 40, my parents thought that having a dog would be too much for Mum. Goldie, our previous dog, had died and we had a new dog Andy who I mostly took for walks. While I was at school Andy was given away to a farm and I cried for days for I wasn't told and didn't even get a chance to say goodbye.

I also didn't want to stop being the baby in the family and was not too nice at the time. However, when my little sister Valerie was born she was adorable and I loved her. Through loving her I became a nicer person.

Playing with Val in the snow. 1962

As a teenager I went to church regularly, but I must admit I enjoyed looking at one particular boy in the choir. I also went to the church Youth Club, where we had great fun. One Sunday the youth club were going on a coach trip to the beach. We went to early morning church before catching the coach. But many of the congregation moaned about us wearing sundresses or shorts to church. The next week our vicar Charlie (Charles de Cerjat) led the service dressed in shorts – we loved him.

Our coach trip was to Weston Super Mare. When we arrived in the coach, we saw a wonderful sandy beach (or so we thought) and wondered why nobody was swimming in the sea and why they were all in the swimming pool. As soon as we could we rushed onto the beach and changed into our bathing suits. We started rushing down the sand towards the sea, only to find that instead of sand it was mud and we started to sink into it. Well, we managed to get out and join all other people in the swimming pool. At that time, we didn't know that this was the Bristol Channel and very muddy. Living in Devon we were used to beautiful sandy beaches.

One evening a boyfriend called for me and I suddenly remembered that I needed to fetch something from my bedroom, which I shared with my sister Eve. I rushed upstairs and went into our bedroom without putting on the light. I passed my sister's bed, stepped over Tiddles the cat, went around my bed, fetched what I wanted and did the return journey out of the room stepping over Tiddles. When I got downstairs, I realised that Tiddles had died some time ago and I had stepped over her spirit.

Tiddles, our cat

About this time, I had a dream which was very real (I don't usually remember dreams unless they have some sort of meaning). I was scared and running through deep snow away from a man. Eventually I reached 'my home' which looked like a roof sticking out the snow. I went down many steps cut into the snow to the entrance door, where the snow had been pushed aside and went inside. Then I was safe. This felt like a cold country, maybe Norway or Sweden. I wondered if this could be a memory of a previous life?

I had another dream where I was walking along Bowden Park Road and had a big white cat with me. I have now recognised this cat as a Snow Leopard who is an Animal Spirit Guide for me.

Chapter 6
Starting Work

When I was 16, I left school at the end of the Summer Term on Friday. On Monday I started my full-time job in an insurance firm. I started as the office junior, working with another girl. At school, we finished the day at 4:00 p.m., but that Monday I had to work until 5:30 p.m. I think that was the longest one and a half hours of my life, I thought the time to go home would never come.

The girl who worked with me was funny and would get me to sing *We're busy doing nothing, working the whole day through* with her quite loudly. There was an older lady who was in charge of the office and her desk was at the other end of the big office. She would hear us and start walking towards us to tell us off and we would gradually sing softer and softer. By the time she got to our desks, we were silent and busy. I think she quite liked us winding her up in this way.

Our office was only girls, 13 of us all working on insurance proposals. As juniors, the other girl and I had to make the tea and coffee at break time. We would go into the kitchen and she would get the kettle lead and switch the power on at the plug and direct the lead towards me. I felt afraid because I thought the electricity could come out and hit me, so used to run around the kitchen away from her. When I think back, this seems so very silly.

Next door was an office for insurance claims and this was mostly males. Sometimes I had to deliver some papers to this office and remember that I used to feel so self-conscious, because at that time I was very shy.

On Fridays there was a huge post and I was in charge of this. There would be 33 envelopes, one for each of the insurance agents, plus all the other post. Often the other girls would finish their work and come and help. This was very nice of them, but they would come and say, “I’ll do this Pam” and someone else would say “I’ll do that” but I would get confused and not know what I still had to do. After work, I had to take this huge post to the post office.

On one particular Friday, I came out of the post office feeling extremely stressed and thought *what can I do to calm me down*. Well at that time, cigarettes it was said, calmed you down, so I walked up Royal Parade and bought a packet of 10 cigarettes and a box of matches from the kiosk there. I got to my bus stop and felt I couldn’t wait for a cigarette to calm me, so got out a cigarette, put it in my mouth, lit the match and while trying to light the cigarette I burnt the end of my nose. Oh dear. Sadly, I continued to smoke from that day until I was 38 when I finally gave up.

Another incident at work was when a farmer came in and not one of us in the office could understand him. He lived on Dartmoor and spoke in a broad Devonshire accent. It wasn’t until he made a drawing of a tractor that we realised he wanted to insure his tractor. We thought it hilarious.

When any girl had a birthday it was the office tradition to go out in the dinner hour with other girls and go to three pubs in the city centre. At each pub you had to have a different alcoholic drink. Girls didn't drink beer then, so I remember having whisky and orange, port and lemon and vodka and black. We would be sloshed but happy and we always managed to do our work okay in the afternoon.

Chapter 7
A Hard Time

I was brought up to be a good girl and to stay a virgin until I married and I wanted to be a virgin for my husband of the future. And of course, I, just like every other young girl, wanted to fall in love, get married and live happily ever after. Even so, I enjoyed flirting and dating throughout my teenage years and went out on many dates.

That was until at 19 I was raped. I was pulled into a field, tripped up, held down and it was a forced rape. When I am scared I cannot scream, instead, I am quite literally petrified. I kept quiet about being raped, due to embarrassment, until I found that I was pregnant.

I had a really hard time telling my mum and dad, but after the initial shock, they were both really supportive of me. I knew right from the start that I could never have an abortion or give my child away. When I felt my baby move I knew I loved my child. Pregnancy as a single girl in 1966 was hard, with neighbours peeking out of their windows at me, but I held my head high, poked out my tummy and got on with it.

While expecting my baby, I had a dream in which I was walking along Fort Austin Avenue with a friend from schooldays. We were opposite Widey Lane, when she wanted to kill me by stabbing me with a knife. A grave was already in the grass verge. I can't remember if she succeeded in killing me, but not long after my baby was born.

I had to go into hospital because my ankles were swollen with toxaemia (pre-eclampsia). For a week I had to lie or sit in the bed with my feet up. I was a bit overdue and I suppose they needed beds, so my waters were broken to start the birth at about 1:00 p.m. on October 3. I immediately had severe pains in my stomach, so had injections for this in my bottom. However, they didn't seem to work for ages, but it couldn't have been that long. They asked me if I had eaten my dinner, which would give me the strength to push. I said no as it had been liver and I just cannot eat that. So, I had to have a needle with an intravenous line in the back of my left hand to supply me with glucose energy.

They thought that it would be a long time before I needed to push, however, they soon found that my baby had decided to come quickly. They rushed me to the delivery room and the pain injection must have been working by then, as all I can remember is that I mustn't move my left hand with the intravenous drip, or the needle will hurt me. My baby daughter was born at 4:20 p.m. and was gorgeous.

My baby daughter was beautiful and I named her Stephanie. I hadn't found a second name that I liked, but when I held her in my arms, I felt such a joy, that her second name became Joy.

Together with my baby, Stephanie Joy.

After the birth, the doctors were puzzled as they found a lump in my stomach. Several doctors and student doctors came and prodded and poked my stomach. This was the '60s and they didn't ask permission to do so, it was if you were a piece of meat. Then they stood at the end of my bed muttering quietly to each other and after much deliberation they decided it was a Dermoid Cyst. They didn't explain anything to me, but I had strained to hear what they were saying but only heard Dermoid Cyst.

That evening the Night Sister found me crying. I explained that I didn't know what a Dermoid Cyst was and I was frightened. She sat with me and gently told me that I should have been a twin, but that while in my mum's womb my twin had gone inside me. This twin had not grown properly and had become a Dermoid Cyst, a mixture of bone, skin etc. She told me it would probably mean an operation to have it removed. So this explained why I was such a heavy baby when I was born, I was actually two babies.

I had started breastfeeding my daughter but had to change to bottle feeding her so that my mum could look after her while I had an operation to investigate this cyst and also another operation to have it removed.

As far as I knew the operation was successful when I groggily woke in the ward. However, suddenly I was being whisked back to the operating theatre as I was bleeding heavily. My mother and father were called by the hospital as it seems I would possibly die. Maybe I did, all I remember is going along a very white corridor with people all dressed in white. There was no colour anywhere, just white. Did I die for a short while? It seems possible.

Anyway, I did survive and am grateful for the operation because my mum and dad were told that if this Dermoid Cyst had not been removed it would have killed me within approximately two years. The reason for this was that the cyst was growing and would take over my liver. Nothing could be done for the liver at that time.

How grateful am I? Very grateful for if I had not been raped and had not become pregnant, the cyst would not have been found and I would have died. And of course, I would not have had my wonderful loving daughter Stephanie.

They did trace the man who raped me, but I was scared to go to court having been told that if I wore black bra or knickers, I would be considered to be enticing men. Because of this, I would not press charges.

As a consequence of this, I received no benefits and had to go to work as an Accounts Clerk for a large garage to provide for my daughter and I. We lived with my parents and my mum looked after Stevie (Stephanie) during the day and I looked after her for the rest of the time. One night when my daughter Stevie was a baby, she scared me one evening by staring at something that I could not see.

During another night I could not stop her crying, having changed her, fed her and given her gripe water and anything else I could think of. About three in the morning, I was so tired and exhausted that I remember thinking, *If she doesn't stop crying soon I will throw her out the window*. But as soon as the thought came, I knew that I could never do this because I loved her so. However, it made me realise how easy it can be for other parents to cross the line and mistreat their babies.

As I had to go to work the next day my mother came and took over looking after Stevie. In the morning an abscess in Stevie's ear burst, so it was no wonder she was crying all the time with the pain. My poor baby.

Life was hard as I had to do a full-time job, keep my room clean and do the washing and ironing for Stevie and me, as well as babysit my younger sister. I had to ask my parents if I could go out in the evening. They were good to me and allowed me to go out about twice a week.

Chapter 8
A Full-Time Mum

In 1969 I was working in The Victualling Yard, Stonehouse and met a man, who could be very funny and made me laugh. He asked me out and eventually, I did go out with him. Then he asked me to marry him and I am ashamed to say I laughed. He kept asking me all that evening and I kept laughing, but eventually, he wore me down and I said yes, I would marry him.

So, in January 1970, we got married. There was a reception in the afternoon and then we went to our new home, a downstairs flat. My husband consummated the marriage and then went upstairs to talk to the Landlord and Landlady. He stayed with them for most of the evening watching their television. I was left downstairs, feeling lonely and with no television. We later went to our bedroom which was very cold as it was January and north-facing and we only had cold cotton sheets and two blankets. When we got into bed that night he turned over and went to sleep, not even cuddling me. I ended up very cold and miserable and crying myself to sleep.

Very quickly I became pregnant and while waiting for my baby, I had a dream in which I was walking in the area near Seven Trees Clinic. An ambulance came hurtling down the hill from the hospital and pinned me up against the wall, killing me. Shortly after my gorgeous baby boy was born and we called him Gary.

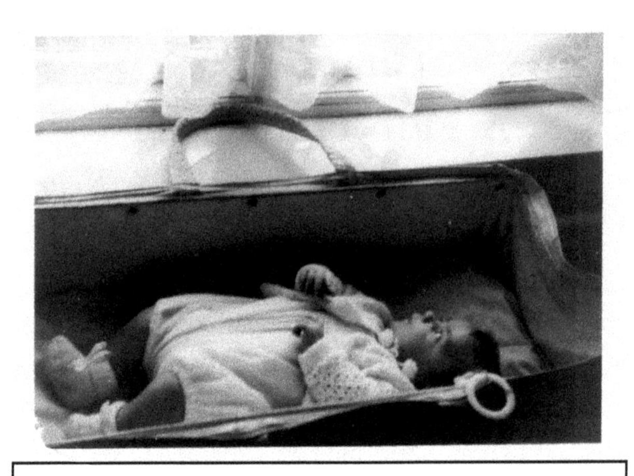

My gorgeous baby Gary

There is a saying that dream of a death, hear of a birth, but I didn't realise that it was going to be my death each time I was due to give birth. However, I am still here to tell the tale and both my children are wonderful and now adults.

I loved Gary to bits, but this did not stop the Baby Blues which turned into depression. I feel the depression was caused by my conditioning to think that I was now committed to being with my husband till death do us part. It was not caused by my beautiful baby boy. This depression lasted for a year and thank goodness for my friend Carol, for she came over most days and took me under her wing. I always looked after my new baby Gary and my daughter Stevie, but I didn't take care of me.

I loved playing with Gary as a baby, something I had really missed with Stevie, as I had had to work when she was little and she would often be asleep when I came home. Gary loved being in company and would not sleep in the bedroom, but as soon as I bought him into the lounge with all the noise, he would fall asleep. When a little bit older he loved to throw his toys out of his playpen and for me to put them back in.

Stevie at four years old was full of questions – how, why, where, what, when and I had difficulty trying to keep her amused. So, I taught her all the nursery rhymes, her alphabet, her numbers, taught her to read a little and told her stories trying to make up for lost time.

Chapter 9
Dark Times

In the flat we lived in I often saw in the lounge the spirit of an old man with a beard sitting in the corner in an armchair (that wasn't there). This man I knew was friendly. I know now that he is a great great grandfather and is a spirit guide for me.

However, one night, quite late, a nephew of my husband came to the door. My husband thought he had been drinking or on drugs, however he had taken neither. He took him into the front bedroom, not liking to bring him down to me in the living room.

This nephew had been dabbling in black magic quite deeply. He claimed that a toy dog which sat on my mother-in-law's bed bit him. He also claimed that a green witch followed him around. Maybe this was all in his head, but he believed it.

This particular night he claimed that he had walked past the high wall outside Beaumont Park and had been called to climb over it into the park. He said he saw the devil. He was extremely frightened and came to us as we lived nearby.

Knowing something was wrong but not what, I just said a simple prayer, "Please God, let me help him." All I can say is that Peace descended on me and I told my husband to fetch him into the living room.

During the night we both talked constantly to him. I had a cross (not consecrated) which we put facing him on the arm of the chair. At first, he couldn't look at it and turned it upside down (supposedly the devil's way). Every time he turned it upside down, we turned it the right way up. Gradually over the night, he was able to keep it the right way up and finally could look at it. Finally, in the early hours of the morning, my husband took the cross and placed it in his left hand and held his hand closed over it. Our nephew claimed it burnt him. I did not see a burn, but I don't think I looked for one. Since then, as far as I know, he has worn the cross and been okay.

My husband said that I was taken over that night as I was quoting many verses in the Bible and acting differently. I do not know if this is true, as I do know some quotations from the bible, but I had certainly felt at peace with absolutely no fear.

A little while after this, Stevie, my young daughter, woke up and wanted a drink of water. I went down the corridor, opened and shut the living room door and then felt I was being watched, I did not like this feeling. It was definitely not the nice man in the armchair. I told myself not to be so silly and went through the other door into the kitchen. I collected a glass of water, opened and shut the door from kitchen to living room, walked a couple of steps and walked through 'something'. I really didn't like the feeling and was petrified. I must have screamed or called, because the next I knew I was in the hallway (having opened and shut the living room/hall door) and my husband was there. I hadn't spilt any of the water.

We checked on Stevie and gave her the water. I went to bed and said what had happened. I prayed and saw a shimmering white shape which at the time I knew was an angel sent to guard us.

I used to go to church on Sundays, so I visited the Vicar, who I thought would help me by cleansing the house. He came to the house but he did not even try to bless or cleanse the house. Instead, he blessed me and only wanted to convert me, thinking I was bad. I did not feel I needed to convert as I already had a strong belief in God, followed the teaching of Jesus Christ and went to Church. However, after this Vicar's visit, I stopped going to Church.

Following this, I asked my dad to help by contacting his best mate Harry through their ESP. So, Dad came and talked to Harry. Dad could see and hear Harry, but neither I nor my husband could see or hear anything. Harry told Dad that the episode with our nephew had opened a door, which allowed a disturbed spirit through. The spirit was a woman who had lost a child and wished to see Stevie. Harry or someone in spirit closed this door and I had no more experiences like this in the flat.

Chapter 10
Ordinary and Extraordinary Times

We moved to a council house in another part of Plymouth where Stevie went to the local Infant School and Gary started nursery school. We had a big garden and the children loved playing there. They had swings and a seesaw, Wendy house, paddling pool and at the top of the garden a trampoline, really it was a mattress which my husband had buried beneath the earth. There were blackberries to pick at the top of the garden and Gary spent many a happy hour saving lots of ladybirds.

Mixed feelings in this house. In bed I often felt that I was touched, either my feet or my forehead being stroked. Although afraid this was not unpleasant. I know now that this is my Guardian Angel.

In this house I frequently smelt apple pie baking in the kitchen, which was fine. I felt watched on the landing and stairs at night. Not a nice feeling. There was a window at the bottom of the stairs which Stevie especially didn't like. She felt there were three nasty faces looking in. Also, Gary said he woke up one night and saw a horrible person like a jester bending over him.

On November 5, we had a bonfire and firework party at our house and everyone had a great time. We came back into the house for a wonderful buffet and party.

In the morning I came downstairs and found on the living room carpet a worm – something I really don't like, as I don't like squidgy and slimy things. I remember using the hand brush and sweeping it into the dustpan and then throwing it out into the garden. Yuk!

My husband became a caretaker at a Methodist church and we moved into a flat on the premises. On church property I felt protected, but everything was still not quite right. My husband ran the Church Youth Club and I also became a Youth Leader. The main room had a table tennis table and darts board and in the snooker room were two large snooker tables. It was here that Stevie, Gary and I learnt to play these games. I still love table tennis, darts and especially snooker to this day.

I began an Art Club at the Youth Club, which was held in a back room through a corridor at the bottom of the building. I really did not like going through the corridor into this room on my own.

While I was a Youth Leader, I did a small course on counselling. We were asked to role play and to sometimes be the one being counselled and if possible, to use a real situation. I thought that I would be young, single and pregnant, easy-peasy I thought having gone through this. And so it was, until one person asked, "How did you feel?" Well, I burst into tears as no one had dealt with my feelings when I really was young and pregnant, only the practicalities at the time. So, it was a very good session all round as it was a real-life counselling session and I felt much better afterwards, having released much emotion after 10 years of unknowingly keeping it inside.

One day my husband and the children came back with a dog they had found scavenging for food. He was very skinny and had been trying to eat a black banana skin. They brought him into the kitchen and he backed into a tiny space between the wall and the cooker as he was terrified. We could not lift our hand in the air as he would duck as though we were going to hit him. We did ask the local radio, newspaper and police if anyone had lost him. No one claimed him and we were thankful as he had obviously been ill-treated previously. We named him Shandy and loved him to bits. He was a greyhound and saluki mix and was very beautiful with sandy coloured hair and feathers of hair on his ears, back of legs and his tail.

My beautiful dog Shandy

While living at this house, I had two outings with my husband. One organised by Carol and her husband for us to join them at the News Ball. Enjoyable until her husband really annoyed her and we left. The other which, surprise surprise, my husband organised for us to go to Bovisand Beach on the bus. An enjoyable day, until we got home and heard the news that the Earl of Mountbatten had been killed.

Other outings with myself and the children were ones where we could walk or catch the bus locally. Other than that, we were extremely lucky that my dad took us to the beach in the summer quite regularly, often down to Trevone which he loved.

During this period my Uncle Ken died and at his funeral, my Aunt Doreen led the way into the church and into the pews. However, she went along to the end of the pew and I ended up sitting in what I considered to be her seat. During the funeral, I felt that my lovely Uncle Ken came past the coffin and towards me and I mentally told him that Aunt Doreen was at the end of the pew.

Since then, at several funerals, I have felt the spirit of the person who died at the funeral ceremony. Often, they seem to wander around to see who is there and are usually happy at the turnout.

One evening Stevie went into her bedroom and saw a silver-grey shape going out through the window. This frightened her very much and I slept with her for quite a while. This was no hardship for me as I absolutely loved being a mum and looking after my children, but I was not happy in the marriage, so was happy not to sleep in the same bed as my husband.

Chapter 11
Annis Horriblis

The year 1982, just seemed to have so much hardship that in the Queen's words it was my year Annis Horriblis.

In the January, my dog Shandy nearly died with distemper and I had to nurse him for a week. Thankfully he survived.

Gary, my son, was knocked over by a car and was raced to the hospital, thankfully he was not too badly hurt, but needed a cut in his head stitched up. I held his hand while this was done and the surgeon thought I was very brave, but I was just being a supportive mum. Gary also had a chip off the bone in his shoulder, but nothing could be done for this. He spent a week in the Royal Naval Hospital in Plymouth and then was allowed home.

My dad, age 63, had been diagnosed with cancer in the trachea, which was inoperable and had been given six months to live. Although he was given treatment, he did die within six months in March 1982.

Mum phoned me when he was dying, but by the time I arrived at the house, Dad was dead. We went to the bedroom to see Dad. Due to the diagnosis of six months, we had already been prepared for Dad's death and were actually glad that he was now out of pain. Mum was very calm and when the phone rang, she went downstairs to answer it.

My lovely Dad

While in the bedroom I felt scared to be with a 'dead body'. I had never seen a dead body before and I moved to the other side of the room even though it was my dad. In my head I seemed to hear Dad say, "Don't be such a nincompoop, it's only me." I don't use the word nincompoop, it is my dad's word, so I knew it was my dad and that he was still here as a spirit. After that, I could kiss him.

I went with Mum to see Dad at the Chapel of Rest. Dad was in the coffin with a white satin pillow and cover. When I looked at Dad, I seemed to hear him say, "Don't I look like a twerp dressed all in white?" Again, twerp is a word my dad used. I know my dad spoke to me on these two occasions.

After this I don't say I believe in the afterlife, I say I know there is an afterlife.

About a month after this my mum was diagnosed with a cancerous lump in her breast. Of course, my sisters and I worried that Mum was going to die as well. She had to go to the hospital to have the breast removed. Mum was obviously afraid and I was afraid that I would lose my mum as well as my dad.

My loving mum at Seaton Beach, Cornwall.

The night before she went to the hospital I stayed with her. In the morning, she told me that Dad had been cuddling her all night long and she felt peaceful and loved.

Then I told her that I had a dream where I came downstairs in my dressing gown and Grampa, who had lived with us for a while before he died, came out of his room at the bottom of the stairs, dressed in his dressing gown and slippers. He gave me the most wonderful cuddle, which I can still feel now. We both felt that Dad and Grampa had come to comfort us both.

Mum had a successful operation to remove her breast and lived to be 95 years of age.

It was also the year of the Falklands War. As we lived in Plymouth, a city full of servicemen, there were constant lorries loaded with troops and equipment passing by on the way to the Dockyard for the naval ships.

Later in the year, I went to a café with my mum for a coffee. We were just generally talking when she suddenly asked me if everything in my marriage was alright. For years I had been answering "fine, fine," but this time I burst into tears because I was not happy being with my husband.

Shortly afterwards I woke up one morning and my husband said that I had been talking in my sleep. I asked if I had said anything interesting. He replied that I had said about suing him for divorce and whether I was thinking about this. I thought I should be truthful and replied yes. So after 12 years of marriage, my children and I moved out and went to stay with my mum until I found other accommodation.

Finally, I moved with the children to the top flat in the biggest house in Cawsand for a winter let. This flat was extremely cold and we had one oil fire to keep us warm. We had been watching the series Tenko and were desperate to watch the next episode. We went into the very large lounge, which was extremely cold and switched the TV on. However, in Cawsand you need a booster to watch TV and all we could see was fuzzy snowy dots.

So, one of us stood very close listening to try and hear what was being said. One stood well back trying to make sense of who was on screen by the movement. However, we did give up because we really couldn't make sense of any of it and it was really cold.

When we first visited, Mum said don't sleep in the big bedroom. Later she said she didn't like the feeling there. But ignoring her we all decided to sleep in one room where there was a double bed for me and Stevie and a single bed for Gary, instead of being in two bedrooms.

One night Stevie and Gary sat together in the double bed playing a game. Then they both fell asleep, so instead of disturbing them, I climbed into the single bed. During the night I woke to a very heavy black feeling, as though an entity was upon me. I could not move. I could not speak. I tried to say the Lord's Prayer but had difficulty remembering it all the way through. After many tries, I managed to say, "And deliver us from evil" and finish the Lord's Prayer and the feeling lifted.

I then called to my children to wake up and put on the light. When they awoke and did this, I was able to get out of the bed and climb in the double bed with them. All three of us slept in this bed that night.

Gary said that he never felt anything while sleeping in the single bed. But I felt later that this entity was a previous butler who preyed on the female servants, so he would not have been interested in Gary, a male.

After that I always felt there was a presence in the flat, especially near the window in the big bedroom and the hallway.

The nights were very dark in the village because there was no street lighting. Stevie and Gary still had to go to school in Plymouth and had to get up really early. They had to leave the house in the dark, catch the bus to Cremyll, get the ferry across and then a bus to school. Obviously, they had the same journey back in the evening, also in the dark.

This became too much, so they stayed with my mum during schooldays and came to Cawsand at the weekends. This meant of course I was on my own in the flat with the entity. I had no idea what to do about it at that time, although I used to ask God and Jesus for protection. I was pleased when we were offered a place in Laira, Plymouth and we could move out of the flat.

In the following January, my younger sister Val fell backwards down the stairs, landing with her spine on the corner of the radiator. She was taken to a hospital in Plymouth where they found she had a spinal cord injury. However, she needed to be taken to Cardiff where there was a hospital, which specialised in spinal injuries. She was in Cardiff for several weeks, but sadly feeling did not come back into her lower body and she was diagnosed as paraplegic.

My sister Val before she fell

What a year or thirteen months to be exact!!!

Chapter 12
Single but Happy

We moved to a lovely maisonette overlooking the river Plym in Laira, Plymouth. My children and I were happy there and we enjoyed watching people rowing, water skiing, windsurfing, etc on the river. In addition, there were many water birds, especially when the tide was out and the mud was showing.

To get to our place, we had to climb a very steep hill. The first time I climbed this hill I stopped at least three times and was very out of breath. By the time I left the area, I was so fit, being able to walk quickly up the hill carrying bags of shopping.

On the Anniversary of Dad's death, Mum came out to spend the day with me and the children. However, I didn't think to ask her to stay overnight. I found out afterwards that Mum was dreading returning to the house. When she got there, she did not really want to go in. But when she opened the door, the house was full of faces of people who loved her and the house was full of love. She said it only lasted a short while but filled her with peace.

I also met a neighbour who became my friend. We went to Aerobics together and had great fun. She worked selling ice-creams from a van. When she was with her ice-cream van outside our home, we would run outside to get ice-creams which she would load with clotted cream on top – delicious.

Stevie, Gary and I would go to the River Plym to have a picnic and Shandy loved lying in the shallow water. I remember one extremely hot day walking back from our picnic and being so hot and tired after a lovely day out.

Pam with Stevie and Gary

Later in the winter, it snowed, enough for us to go sledging. My friend found a large piece of linoleum and we had one sledge and both families set off with Shandy our dog to the park which had a steep slope. Both families were able to climb aboard the linoleum to slide downhill. It was fabulous. My children had not known that in my childhood it had often snowed and I loved sledging. They too loved it as did our dog Shandy who enjoyed sliding down on his own.

I often had feelings of not being alone, but I was not too frightened here. But I have always been afraid of flames and have always worked out a fire escape, wherever I have lived. I have not known why I was afraid of flames and wasn't afraid of smoke that can choke.

One evening we watched a film where a witch was burnt. I had watched several films where witches were burnt at the stake but had not worried about this. However, in this particular film, the witch was tied to a large pole and then lowered onto the flames. This really freaked me, as I felt that I too had done this. I feel that this happened to me in a past life.

Other neighbours of mine often asked if we would like to watch a film with them. They watched various films but often watched frightening horrors, which I never liked. One day after seeing a horror film with them the previous evening I was still feeling a bit shaken. I was doing my ironing at the time and suddenly felt myself growing very big. It felt like my head was at the ceiling. It frightened me and I switched off the iron and sat on the settee. As I sat there a ray of light with golden crosses in it came from the wall to my left and filled me with peace. How beautiful. I was later told that this ray of light was a protection for me.

About this time, I got a job working for the Disability Information & Advice Centre in Plymouth. I loved working here, with my boss and the many volunteers, all of whom had a disability of some sort. I learnt so much in this job and enjoyed the variety of work: finding and giving information; helping the volunteers; training our staff; giving training Devonwide on a computer database and creating other databases, spreadsheets, posters and PowerPoint presentations and also giving talks to all who were interested in the work of the Disability Information & Advice Centre.

Later I visited people in their homes to help them receive benefits and to give much advice.

I used to visit Mum once a week and most times I walked with Shandy, my dog, to Mum's. We had our set route, up to the top of the hill and down the other side. Over the bridge across the Parkway main road and up the next hill to Mum's. This kept me fit as well as enjoying the day with Mum.

One night Shandy ran away and I couldn't find him. I was so worried I hardly slept that night and was so tired when I had to go to work. Mum phoned me at work to say that Shandy had gone to her house. She brought him back to me in my dinner hour and so he had to stay in my office for the afternoon.

My daughter Stevie was now at the College of Art in Birmingham and in her student digs, she had two gerbils as pets. During the summer holidays, she had to go to London to do a work placement. I was looking after the gerbils, who stayed in her bedroom with the door closed. We had a cat Scampy and one morning I got up and found her bedroom door open. The cage for the gerbils was on the floor and the cage door was open. Oh, my giddy aunt where were the gerbils. Had the cat eaten them. I searched and searched and finally found one gerbil. So back in the cage he went and put on top of a cupboard. However, I could not find the other gerbil and I had to go to work.

At work, a friend asked why I was crying and I told her the story of the missing gerbil. She volunteered to take me home in the dinner hour, as she had a car. So back to my home and Stevie's bedroom, where she immediately jumped on the bed. I asked why and she said she was scared of small furry animals. However, while I continued looking under the bed and under other furniture, she kept a lookout and finally spotted a bedraggled gerbil. Thankfully I caught the gerbil and put it back in the cage with the other. Making sure the door was totally closed, we left and went back to work. Looking back this was a very funny incident with her jumping on the bed, but luckily there was a happy ending.

Chapter 13
Getting Connected

I met and fell in love with another man. Stevie was already living away as an art student in Birmingham so when a flat had been found for Gary, who was now a young adult, I moved in with this man and later we married. I saw in my mind's eye an image of my dad and his dad's faces together and thought they looked happy that we were married.

My husband was romantic and always celebrated birthdays, Valentine's and anniversaries. We would usually go for a meal and sometimes to dance. One Valentine's Day he had booked a posh hotel dinner and dance. However, the menu was not the best: Love Apple Soup (tomato soup – which I didn't like), steak Diane (not so bad) and for sweet Queen of Heart Tart and custard (jam tart and custard). And the service was so slow, in fact, at one point I went looking for the waiter. By the time we had finished the meal the dance was over. What a disappointment for us both.

I often had feelings of not being alone, sometimes okay, sometimes frightened. The problem was not knowing who was there. Shandy, our dog, often watched empty space usually at picture height in the lounge and the tap in the kitchen had a habit of turning on at odd times. I heard odd taps and bumps in the house, which didn't seem to belong to our house or next door. I never did like showering or bathing while alone in the house. I always felt watched.

One day while sorting out photos in photo frames, I lost one small photo frame. I searched through all that I had thrown out in case I had accidentally put it in the rubbish. But it wasn't there and after searching the house, I still couldn't find it. A couple of months later, I opened my make-up drawer and there it was, right on top. At that time, I put make-up on every day, so could not possibly have missed the photo frame had it been there previously. I felt that someone in spirit was playing games.

After my dog Shandy died, I frequently thought he was around the house, and I used to feel him. My left leg would go cold, and I felt he was sitting leaning against me as he used to do.

I had a dream one night and dreamt that I was asleep but that I could feel Shandy lying beside me on the bed with his legs poking into my back. In life, he was never allowed upstairs in that house. I knew, in my dream, that Shandy was dead, but I put out my hand to feel him. I could feel him and I was stroking his head, then I opened my eyes and saw him. I was so very happy when I woke up.

In the last few months of 1996, I saw a very real face in the bathroom carpet. This face is the largest I have ever seen and stayed the longest. The most prominent feature was the right eye, but I could see the shape of the face, both eyes, hair and sometimes other features. The face sometimes is friendly, but sometimes seems angry – but not at me.

My husband said he could just about make out a face as I pointed it out. Mum and my friend couldn't see what I did. The name of George seemed to be in my head, but later that changed to the name of Alan Whitcombe. Why, I have no idea. The date of 1878 also seemed to be 'right'.

I drew a picture of the face but didn't do it justice. I took the picture to work and showed a colleague who was psychic. She said that she felt he worked as a woodsman in the woods, probably in Plympton. He did not want me to see his nose as it was broken. She felt he was a sensitive man and that he was drawn to me and did not at that time want to move on.

After this, I 'talked' with Alan and asked if he had a wife and children. I also talked about whether he wanted to see his mother and father and all his family hoping that this would get him to consider moving on.

I then saw a programme on the television about ghosts in which there was a pub in Devon, near Torbay where there was a ghost of a young man, who was a biker. They called in a psychic who was a clergyman. He contacted the young man, made a circle of light which was a pathway to the other side and asked the young man to step into the circle. When he did, the psychic prayed and asked that the young man be able to pass through. The young man did.

In the morning I felt that I was being asked (not by Alan, but by someone else who was perhaps guiding me) to try this circle and pray for Alan to pass on. I did make the circle and prayed that Alan be allowed to pass on. I seemed to feel Alan leave, but as he did, I thought he said *Thank you. I love you.* I think the *I love you* was in the sense of loving friends.

I spoke with my colleague later in the morning, telling her what I had done. She felt I had done the right thing. While talking with her, I suddenly felt great emotion –

overwhelming ecstatic happiness and I cried with joy. She said that this was Alan sending his thanks to me.

After this, I began to feel 'presences' in the house even more and see movements at the side of my vision. I felt sometimes that someone stood very close to me. On occasions, when I was feeling braver, I put my hand where I thought the presence was and could feel a tingling in my hand.

One night while my husband was working a night shift, I woke up and saw a short old man with a flat cap standing on the other side of the bed and just looking at me. I was not at all frightened by this as it was a very loving presence. Some weeks later I was looking through old photos with my mum and there was the man. It was my great grandfather who was nicknamed Old Fa.

Old Fa, my great grandfather.

My husband and I went on holiday to Brittany via the ferry and visited many places, as we travelled in a circular route around the area. We were in a hotel near Benodet eating our evening meal when my husband overheard an Irish voice at the next table saying how he had enjoyed his Guinness at the pub. He needed to know more and spoke with this gentleman to find out where this pub was.

So, after dinner, off we went. As soon as he asked for a Guinness and the barman realised we were English, we were made so welcome. It was suggested that I try Kir et Cassis (wine with blackcurrant liquor) and I can assure you it was very nice indeed. Students and the locals wanted to talk to us and practice their English. While we talked throughout the evening the drinks were constantly filled. At the end of the evening, we went to pay the bill and were told that the drinks had all been paid for. How wonderful and how lovely of the person or persons who paid for our drinks.

Well, we went outside and the cold air hit us. I have no recollection of the journey back to the hotel, but when we got there, we had to go up some steps outside. I can remember crawling up these steps. How disgusting, but I had had a very good evening.

We also went to visit the Chateau of the Duchesse Anne in Dinan. It was all very interesting until we went down some stairs to the crypt. About the third step from the bottom, I just froze and did not want to move. I felt something bad and thought a duel had taken place there and one had died. It took a lot of courage to move on down. I really did not want to go back up the stairs again, but of course, it was necessary.

Back home we often went out as we had joined the local social club. Most Saturday evenings when possible we would visit the club, where both my husband and I loved to meet up with friends. We also loved to dance, particularly the jive.

In our lounge, there was a plant hanging from the stairs and this had one long strand. We moved the furniture around so the settee was across the room and easier to watch the television. This meant that the path from the main door to the kitchen was past this plant. It was nigh on impossible to go past without knocking the strand and making it swing.

On two separate occasions, when I was alone in the house and sitting on the settee the strand started swinging as though someone had just walked by. I could not make this strand swing by blowing it or any other means.

I often wished I was psychic enough and brave enough to see who was there.

When on holiday in Paphos, Cyprus I had a few psychic incidents. My husband and I were going around Nao Paphos (an old Greek/Roman city) when I suddenly felt I had a friend with me – a friend from the time of the city. At the small amphitheatre someone called, “Pam, come and sit here by us,” and I felt that I had to sit on one particular seat. Although called by my present name, I felt that perhaps I had lived here before – as an Egyptian girl. I felt ‘my friends’ were Greek, not Egyptian. I also felt compelled to climb some steps – that are now overgrown and don’t go anywhere in particular.

Since then, I just seem to know that my father at that time was an Egyptian merchant trader and sometimes we lived in Nao Paphos and sometimes in Alexandria, Egypt. I would love to visit Alexandria one day.

At the Tombs of the Kings, it was like blocks of tombs and we went into several tombs. However, I got really spooked in a tomb in block number three. I really didn’t like the feeling there at all and couldn't wait to get out. It almost felt like it could have been my tomb.

While on the way to the Baths of Aphrodite, I needed to go to the toilet and so we stopped in a small town. There were two cubicles and the toilet was empty. I did what I needed to do and was washing my hands when a lady came into the toilet and I wondered why she didn't go into a cubicle, as I knew she was standing behind me. When I turned around there was nobody physically there.

We also went to Colossi Castle, which is approximately from the Crusader period. Just inside the main door was a Christian mural. I was standing looking at this mural when I felt that someone (I think a man) was standing behind me. Again, there was no one physically there.

In May 1997 I went to see my friend Carol in Cornwall. We talked about her mother, who she really missed I was told to say that her mum loved her. I also 'heard' – red spotted dress and baby boots – both of which meant something to Carol. In addition, there was Farthing Hill – Carol said there was a Penny Hill near where they had lived and that she used to play a game with farthings with her mother.

In this second marriage of mine, after several years, I realised that although romantic, he often used to put me down and often in front of friends. We did have many good times together, especially on birthdays and on holidays. But after the last holiday in Cyprus, where he was not so nice and after being together for 13 years I had had enough and decided to leave.

Chapter 14
My Path at Last

When my marriage with husband number two ended, a male friend and volunteer co-worker who I had always got on well with asked me out We did go out together and eventually we become partners. I realised later that we were soul mates. We found a small, terraced house in Saltash with a fantastic view along the River Tamar. I often came home from work and sat with a coffee on the bench in the garden to relax and just admire the view.

Since a child, I have always seen faces on walls, carpets, trees, etc, often with several different faces appearing in the same spot, as though jostling for space.

While living in Saltash this became more frequent and I saw several faces, especially on the bathroom carpet. Some were very pronounced and others were more indistinct. Sometimes faces were over faces. Sometimes I saw a face very clearly, looked away briefly and then the face I had been looking at was gone and another one was there. Some faces stayed and some disappeared. The faces I saw were very real.

When I draw a face from my imagination, the face is very obviously fictitious and not real and in addition, always faces to the left.

Here are pictures of faces from my imagination, which always face the same way.

I drew several of the faces on the carpet and every face was an individual, definitely not my imagination. I tried to see other things other than faces – to see if this was just my imagination. However, no matter how hard I try, I could not see flowers, objects, etc. Here are some of the faces I drew.

Occasionally I saw animals. I did see Shandy, my dog, but this soon faded. I also saw two horses, but each in association with a man sitting on the horse's back.

I wondered why I saw faces. *Were they spirits who were stuck here, who wished to reach the 'other side'?* I wondered. *Or were they spirits from the 'other side' visiting?* Maybe they were both.

When I felt it appropriate, I would ask God and the angels to help me make a circle of light to be a pathway to the other side and ask any spirit who needed help to step into the circle of light. I prayed and asked that anyone who wished to pass over, would be helped.

If this is a spirit visiting I wondered how am I supposed to contact the person to whom they wish to talk? Who will this help? Maybe this is something that is still in the development stage and my spirit guides will let me know how when I am ready.

My man and I married in Torpoint and had a fabulous honeymoon in Turkey. I became stepmother to his children and enjoyed being a second mum to them.

We moved to another house back in Plymouth and again I could see faces in the carpets and particularly in the bathroom. Only one face seemed to stay and appeared to be a fisherman, as he was dressed in yellow wet weather gear, hat and Macintosh. I found out that this fisherman was a spirit guide for me called Ben. I now know that this is the man I saw in my very first flat, where he used to sit in an armchair and smile at me, a loving energy.

My place of work needed a new Project Manager and interviews were being held. I had gone out in my dinner hour to read and sit in the sun. I got too hot and came back into the building. In the reception was a lady waiting to be interviewed. I spoke to the Receptionist saying something about how hot it was and how it was too hot to stay out and this lady joined in the conversation. As soon as I turned to her, I knew I wanted her for my boss. She is a soul mate and again it was like a recognition.

She did become my boss and we became friends. Now we do not work with each other, but we are still great friends and always will be.

I wanted to know more about psychic and spiritual things and asked a friend to go to a spiritual evening with me. I wanted a reading, but I only had £20 and most of the Card Readers cost £30 or more. But there was one lady charging £20, so I had my card reading with her. One of the things she said was that I was ready to spiritually move on and needed to join a circle or group.

At the end of the evening, I asked if she knew of a group I could join. She said she was thinking of starting a group and gave me her telephone number. “Phone me in a fortnight,” she said. I couldn’t wait for that fortnight to pass and to phone her.

So, in 2001, she started a spiritual development and meditation group to which I went and from then on I have never looked back. I fell in love with everything and thought meditations were wonderful. I had found what I had been looking for and was hooked. I was now definitely Drawn to the Light and on my Spiritual Path and I couldn’t wait to learn more.

Ingram Content Group UK Ltd.
Milton Keynes UK
UKHW020639220623
423865UK00011B/581